Kaizen

The Kaizen Way of Continuous Improvement in Personal and Professional life

Jason Bennett & Jennifer Bowen

Table of Contents

Introduction

Over so many decades, the Japanese people have come to be associated with excellence, innovation, efficiency (c'mon, aren't the most fuel-efficient cars in the world Japanese?), resiliency and economic success.

And why not? From the ashes of defeat after World War 2 and with very little by way of natural resources, they were able to rise to become the world's second biggest economy next only to the juggernaut that's the United States - at least before the sleeping economic giant that is China woke up.

Today, Japan is still one of the top 3 to 5 economic powerhouses in the world. And that's a testament to the Japanese way of doing things.

All of us can learn how to succeed in life through Japan's philosophies and culture. They've walked the talk and now, their walk is doing the talking. And if there's one Japanese philosophy that we all would benefit much from learning, it's the Kaizen philosophy of continuous improvement.

And in this book, we'll take a look into this amazing Japanese philosophy and how we can apply it to our personal and professional lives to be more successful.

In particular, we'll be looking at the key principles of this amazing philosophy so the philosophy can come alive in practical ways, which can make it easier for us to apply in daily life.

If you're ready, turn the page so we can begin!

Chapter 1 - Why Continuous Improvement?

"Rome wasn't built in a day, but they were busy laying bricks by the hour." - John Heywood, English playwright

I want you to imagine one of the 7-wonders of the world, the Egyptian pyramids. I haven't been there personally, but the people I knew who have would tell me pictures don't do justice to the pyramids' grandeur.

The size, the symmetry - you just knew that these grand creations (man-made or otherwise) weren't put up as fast as you can cook food in a microwave oven.

It doesn't take a genius to figure out that to be able to build something as massive and as enduring as the Egyptian pyramids, lots of work and time were needed.

It's the same with personal and professional accomplishments, i.e., we can't just experience them with one, two, or three drops of hard and smart work. No - it takes an accumulation of productive actions over time to achieve meaningful successes in any areas of our lives.

And often times, even our previous successes don't mean much after a year or two unless we continue to build on them. This is because not only do we live in a world where change is the only permanent thing but the world we live in now has never been as dynamic or fast-changing as it is today.

In other words, we need to be able to adapt to our world's ever-changing requirements if we want to experience consistent and massive successes in the most important areas of our lives.

And the only way to adapt to a world whose benchmarks or standards for success continue to change is to continuously improve.

There's just no other way. Allow me to give a practical example of this truth.

Aunt Ning

My Aunt Ning is old now and as such, she's pretty much set in her ways and personal changes, if any, are practically "taboo" to her. And that's understandable because at her age and condition, adapting to today's modern world - especially if there's no need for it - can be as difficult for her as it is to bench-press 300 pounds with a body weight of only 100 pounds.

But life can have a way of "forcing" people to improve even if they don't want to. Aunt Ning was ok with using an old-school brick phone, also called a candy bar phone.

You know, those phones that still use actual keypads instead of a touchscreen. She was also never into the Internet, including emails and the like. If it were up to her, she'd be happy just using a brick phone and being offline.

Then phone manufacturers started phasing out brick phones and focused entirely on touchscreen phones.

Because she could no longer get a new brick phone after her last one died, she had no choice but to learn how to use a smart phone. And in the process of upping up her "game," she also learned how to use - and love - the Internet, especially Facebook and YouTube!

These improvements in her life enabled her to enjoy life even more by now being able to connect with friends and relatives from faraway places on an almost daily basis, which she couldn't do with the off-line phones of the past.

And more than just being able to connect with more and more of her friends and relatives, she was also able to learn much more things such as recipes and homemade cures for common ailments, which she was able to share with her own family.

A small change in her life, which was learning how to use a smartphone, opened up so many other small changes that added up to make her life a much joyful and fulfilling one today.

Had she decided to defy change and refused to improve herself by learning how to use a smartphone, she wouldn't have been able to enjoy the beautiful successes in her life personal life that were only possible through learning to use a smartphone and consequently, the Internet.

Lasting Success

There's a reason why rock bands like Metallica continue to fill up stadiums today decades after their mainstream-busting album Black came out in the 1990s and rock bands like Dokken are no longer around.

That reason is continuous improvement. Metallica paid close attention to the changes that were happening not just in the music industry but with technology as well. They leveraged on it by learning how to "improve" the songs and albums they were coming out with in accordance with what their fans and the general rock-music audiences wanted.

They also learned how this thing called "multi-media" works, embraced it, and exploited it to their advantage. How many bands - or even solo artists - do you know whose concert attendees include 40-plus year-old fathers and their teenaged sons?

Because Metallica didn't rest on their laurels and continued to improve their music and multimedia presence, they continue to rock out to sold-out stadiums after more than 37 years in the business!

There's nothing much to say about Dokken, really. The fact that you don't even know of them speaks of how much premium they placed on continuous improvement.

And if you and I want to be more like Metallica in terms of massive and lasting personal and professional success, we need to embrace continuous improvement with open arms - and keep it there!

Chapter 2 - The Kaizen Way

The Japanese - God bless their great nation - have a unique philosophy on continuous improvement, which is called Kaizen. The word is a combination of two Japanese words: "kai," which means change, and "Zen" meaning good. In simple terms, kaizen means, "changing for the better."

In the business world, Kaizen is a way by which an organization's activities are grouped together using the principles of economy, order, discipline, and common sense. In many businesses that have lean production or manufacturing processes, Kaizen is an indispensable part and substantial contributor.

Kaizen pertains to undertakings that seek to improve business processes or functions on a continuing basis and involves everyone in an organization from the chief executive officer all the way down to the lowest ranking employee or volunteer.

In Japan, it's normal to call any technique that improves the way businesses are run as "Kaizen."

Kaizen and Your Personal and Professional Success

Success is all about being able to accomplish goals both big and small. However, some goals are just too big to go at one swing, which can be quite overwhelming.

They can be so daunting that merely taking the first step towards accomplishing them can be so intimidating that the temptation to procrastinate or completely ditch such a goal can become so strong.

Very big goals, which include very rapid and radical personal and professional changes, may initially sound good but when you really think about it, can, make people even more resistant to necessary changes. If you insist on having very big and lofty goals, your chances of experiencing successful and continuous self-improvement are much lower and become discouraged from continuing.

Also, you'll need significantly more resources to succeed with very large goals. And finally, life can throw so many curveballs that can make it harder and harder to successfully accomplish very large goals, let alone accomplish several on a continuing basis.

It's for these reasons why Kaizen involves making small and continuous improvements to your life's most important areas, from personal to professional. With smaller but continuous improvement goals, your chances of success are much, much higher.

Even better, such small changes accumulate and compound over time resulting in more meaningful improvements, much like how compounding interest works.

We'll talk about the power of incremental changes in more detail in Chapter 3.

The History of Kaizen

The story that is Kaizen began when Toyota Motors in Japan started to apply the concept of "quality circles" in its car-production processes, which as partly influenced by teachings of management gurus who have visited Japan after the Second World War.

A quality circle refers to a group of employees or workers with similar or identical duties and responsibilities that regularly convene to identify, evaluate, and address work-related challenges.

This concept garnered a lot of buzz in the Japanese business sector during the 1950s and to this day, the concept of the quality circles or Kaizen groups continues to be practiced in Japan.

The Kaizen business philosophy and practice was popularized the world over thanks largely to Masaaki Imai's works. He was a prominent management consultant and organizational theorist in Japan and was popularly known by his works on quality management, which prominently included the Kaizen practice.

He started to introduce the Kaizen way of business productivity to companies in the west by putting up the Kaizen Institute Consulting Group or KICG. Today, KICG's teams have conducted Kaizen courses and implemented Kaizen methodologies to practically all types of businesses the world over.

And because the Kaizen philosophy's been successfully applied to all kinds of businesses, there's no doubt that we can apply it to our own personal and professional lives as well.

Kaizen Blitz or Event

Kaizen blitzes or events refer to the activities that aim to solve or address specific productivity problems or challenges by employing the Kaizen philosophy. Kaizen events are development projects that are so focused that they can come up with breakthrough improvements within a very brief period of time.

And by "brief" I mean an average of two to ten days. For Kaizen events to be able to accomplish such meaningful results in short periods of time, they need three things: a very clear and concise goal, readily available resources, and fast results.

When these three things are present, Kaizen events can produce meaningful, clear, motivating, and satisfying results.

On a personal note, Kaizen events will refer to our personal endeavors or activities that have very clear goals, which are supported with the necessary tools and resources and can provide meaningful results that will allow us to accumulate many smaller improvements or "victories" en route to bigger personal successes.

Key Kaizen Principles

To effectively implement Kaizen in our lives, we'll need to learn its foundational principles, which will guide us when we embark on continuous improvement endeavors. These principles are:

- *Continuous Improvement*: Companies that implement Kaizen in their business communicate to the world that as an organization, they don't rest on their laurels, i.e., they will not succumb to the temptation of believing that they've already a "good enough" level of service or product and in the process, become complacent. Kaizen-adopting companies are always looking for ways to improve - even in the smallest ways.

  On a personal level, be it with our relationships, personal growth, or professional endeavors, we can apply the same principle to experience massive success in life. If we'll be honest with ourselves, we know that all of us aren't perfect and as such, there'll always room for improvement, however, small such improvements may be. Heck, even people like Bill Gates, Elon Musk, and Oprah Winfrey continue to work on themselves despite their already very lofty statuses in life because they know deep within that they can't rest on their laurels if they want to continue being very successful in what they believe they're called to do in life.

— *Getting Rid Of Antiquated Practices:* One of the biggest reasons why many people and organizations become complacent and aren't able to continue improving is because they hold on to practices and traditions that are antiquated, i.e., outdated and are no longer relevant or working as effectively as expected.

One such company was Netscape. If you're not familiar with Netscape, it's because it's already dead! And why did it die a rather quick death after achieving the pinnacle of success as the world's primary web browser development company? It became complacent and hung on to antiquated practices that no longer served their markets as efficiently as its primary competitor back then, which was Microsoft. And guess who's still around the block and still making hay because the sun continues to shine on them? That's right - Microsoft! And the reason why they're still very much alive and kicking is because they continue to seek ways to improve and in the process, continue to stay very relevant to their customers.

On a personal level, we also need to get rid of antiquated practices or beliefs, the latter is what leading self-help guru Vishien Lakhiani of Mindvalley calls "brules" or b$llsh!% rules. These practices or beliefs, while they may have served us very well in the past, are no longer applicable or relevant today to the point that they aren't just not serving their purpose but they're hindering us from fulfilling ours. One brule or antiquated practice is using a pager. What's the point of using it

14

when the technology supporting it no longer exists? Many people stopped using it simply because the death of its supporting technology forced them to stop but if such technology was still alive, chances are that some people would continue using it despite the availability of more efficient devices.

— *Proactivity*: The term "proactive" was popularized by the late, great self-help guru Stephen Covey in his groundbreaking bestselling self-help book "The 7 Habits of Highly Effective People." In it, he defined the word proactive as having the initiative to do things without being told or being compelled to by exigencies. He also defined the word as having the attitude of accountability, i.e., taking responsibility for one's actions, the results of such actions, and his or her situation. Instead of saying "It's not my fault that I'm poor - I was born into a very poor family!" we can say, "I may have been poor, but if I die poor, it's on me."

Why is being proactive a crucial principle in the Kaizen philosophy? It's because if every person in an organization deflects his or her responsibilities at work, how will the organization move and get things done? If people need to always make excuses for procrastinating or failing to fulfill their responsibilities, organizations will just be throwing precious resources away and end up not being able to accomplish the things they need to. And because continuous improvements often involve things that are not yet urgent or don't appear to be important as of that moment, it takes proactivity to consistently go after them. And if people don't take responsibility for them in the organization, no one will do their part.

For the same reasons, we need to develop a proactive attitude if we're to successfully and consistently apply the philosophy of Kaizen in our lives and eventually, experience massive success in both our personal and professional lives. We can't afford to wait for some exigency to compel us to "level up" because by then, incremental changes may no longer suffice and only radical, one-time-big-time changes may work, which are much harder to accomplish.

— *Never Take New Methods For Granted*: If one of the principles of Kaizen is ditching antiquated practices and beliefs, it doesn't imply that the latest ones will automatically work or be much better than the old ones. Remember, antiquated doesn't necessarily mean "old" - it implies something's no longer relevant, applicable, or effective based on current circumstances. But old practices and beliefs can continue to be relevant and effective, such as the age-old practice of honoring our parents or not stealing. Even if more and more people are treating their parents like crap, it doesn't mean we should readily adapt such a new and "modern" belief and practice it because simply put, it's just not relevant, effective or right.

A very practical example of this principle was my recent purchase of an app called Recastly. It was an app that was promoted as a revolutionary new way of creating marketing videos that can really help draw in more leads for your online marketing efforts. It was an app that automatically generates sub-titles for your videos, which is a very helpful feature when it comes to online marketing videos.

But while it was new and revolutionary, I found it to be a waste of both my time and money because it hardly ever worked for the 4 months that I used it and worse, customer support replies after an average of about 3 weeks per message. At the end of the day, I compelled them to refund me and I had to go back to old school style of generating subtitles for marketing videos. The new failed to trump the old and the old still crushes the new, in that instance.

— *Correct The Wrongs*: Continuous improvements will involve errors along the way. In fact, it's often through errors that we'll know what things we'll need to improve on. That's why Kaizen-companies take process or transactional errors or glitches seriously - they provide insights for further improvements.

It's no different with our personal and professional lives. Things can - and will - go wrong along the way. The key to handling them well is perspective: will we look at errors, mistakes and failures as such or as opportunities for continuous improvement? Our perspective can make a huge difference. If we look at "wrongs" as failures, chances are we may become more discouraged than encouraged and when that happens, we may not take any action to correct them as soon as possible. But if we look at them in the same way we do free lunches, i.e., opportunities to seize, then we will be encouraged and be stoked to work on them as soon as we can so we can continue making improvements that will further build up on our personal and professional successes.

— *Empower Others To Speak*: Kaizen-practicing companies are able to successfully improve their business processes and bottom lines consistently because they have access to goldmines of ideas for continuous improvement. And how are they able to access such goldmines? By empowering everybody in their organization to speak up and provide potentially important information that can help the organization continue making improvements to their processes or fix long-standing challenges. It doesn't mean everybody's opinions will be acted upon. It just means these organizations acknowledge everybody's potential to provide information or suggestions that can enable the organization to solve existing challenges or continue to make improvements

We can do the same in our personal lives even if we don't have a company or employees under us. We can empower the people closest to us to speak up when needed so we can continue making incremental changes or improvements in various areas of our lives that can add up to our personal and professional successes. They can include our parents, our siblings, our closest friends, our work colleagues - especially those we think are always trying to get on our nerves. While it can be quite irritating to hear from such work colleagues or from people who seem to be very critical to us, they can be goldmines for self-improvement information because they don't have any desire to kiss our butts and get into our good graces. As such, we can be assured that at the very least, they're not pulling any punches that can help us become much better people.

More than just being goldmines for information on the things where we can make improvements, we can also empower others to speak up in terms of ideas on how to implement improvements or changes that we've already identified as important. We can think of this as crowdsourcing of implementation ideas. People who aren't directly involved have a higher chance of providing objective ideas and perspectives on how to best implement important changes or improvements in our lives.

- *Ask Why Five Times*: Prior to finalizing any important decisions, we must ensure that such decisions can really address the root issue or challenge we're facing that needs to be addressed through improvements. Often times, we don't get to the root causes because we stop asking prematurely. To ensure a very high degree of success in terms of fleshing out root issues or challenges, asking "why" (five times) can become a very good way to learn. Often times, the real root causes of issues and challenges are uncovered after asking "why?" at least three to five times. And nothing else can optimize our chances of making meaningful incremental changes than knowing the areas of our lives that really need to be addressed and nothing else can derail our self-improvement efforts by barking at the wrong tree due to inability to address the root causes of issues and problems.

- *Economy*: Being able to consistently make incremental changes or improvements in our lives require that we have enough resources for them. That's why it's important that the incremental improvements we make in our lives are economical, i.e., cost-efficient. What good will it do if our personal finances suffer in the name of self-improvement? And when you look at how Kaizen's applied by businesses, cost-cutting or saving more money is often at the heart of such improvements.

  Cutting down on unnecessary expenses is almost always a continuing self-improvement effort because many of the things we need to do in life require having enough funds. Whether it's to get into excellent health and fitness or being able to leave our children a good inheritance, money's needed. And the more money we're able to save, the more resources we can have for continuing self-improvement whether it's in our personal lives (relationships, personal growth, etc.) or our professional lives (business, work, investments, etc.).

— *Never Stop*: As I write this, a thought just popped into my head: the theme song of any Kaizen practitioner, whether an individual or a company, should be Bon Jovi's hit song Sleep When I'm Dead. This is because that's what Kaizen's all about - continuous improvements, however small, for as long as we're alive. Nobody's perfect and as such, there'll always be room for improvement. And if we never stop improving, opportunities for greater personal and professional success won't be far behind.

Of Wastes

The Kaizen philosophy attempts to achieve perfection - the key word being "attempt" - by getting rid of waste in one's workplaces. This means that the ultimate goal of Kaizen is to optimize productivity with little to no wastages by standardizing processes and activities and more importantly, always continuing to improve them.

And speaking of workplace wastes or gemba muda, some of them include:
- Delays;
- Excess inventory;
- Over-processing, or spending more time than necessary on an activity or process;
- Activities that aren't only unnecessary but are also damaging or detrimental to the producer or the process; and
- Defects.

While these "wastes" are in the context of manufacturing or business settings, these can also be placed within the context of our personal and professional situations. Here's how we can do that:

- Delays: These can refer to things that keep us from being able to accomplish things on time such as the habit of procrastination and not giving ourselves extra commuting time to work or other appointments that can cause us to get there late.

- Excess Inventory: This can refer to things like our body weight, which can make us feel lethargic or heavy enough to be significantly less productive and even sick, and having too many commitments that spread us too thin.

- Over-Processing Or Spending More Time Than Necessary On An Activity Or Process: This can refer to situations that are taking more time than what we budgeted for such as when we submit a very hastily and poorly written report to our boss and he requires us to rewrite the whole thing because it's so poorly written to the point it's hard to make sense of it. This means we can end up spending twice the amount of time working on it compared to taking the time to self-edit the thing before submitting it.

- Detrimental Activities: These refer to those that can result in economic, emotional, or personal wastage or loss such as going to the club on weeknights when there's work the next morning, or when we choose to keep our Facebook or YouTube apps on while working on an urgent and very important report that needs to be submitted in a couple of hours.

- Defects: These can refer to sloppy or poorly done work that requires much remedial action that can set us back significantly in terms of turn-around time or money.

When done properly and consistently, Kaizen can - through different self-improvement endeavors - can help us minimize such wastes in our personal and professional activities.

Success - whether in our personal or professional lives - require a great deal of productivity, which is the ability to get more things done for less because all of us have the same amount of time every day.

The key to both successes is to accomplish more within the same 24 hours than most other people and we can only do that when we reduce wastages in our lives to the least possible level.

Chapter 3 - Incremental Change and Innovation

The Kaizen philosophy of continuous change is hinged upon the concept of making incremental change and innovation on a continual basis, which is the opposite of what other "experts" vouch for, which is radical innovation or improvements. So why does Kaizen promote incremental change?

Rome Wasn't Built In A Day...

"...but they were busy laying bricks by the hour." is how the complete saying goes. Something as grand as Rome or the Egyptian pyramids took so many years to complete. For a modern example, take a look at the Burj Khalifa, which is the world's tallest building today. Or take a look at any building in the central business district.

They weren't assembled together in one fell swoop. They were put up in increments, i.e., one section at a time. Obviously, the glass panels and the expensive lavatories couldn't have been installed until the basic frameworks were constructed, which couldn't have been done had the foundations weren't established yet.

If we're to compare our personal and professional successes to buildings and pyramids and civilizations, it's clear that the best way to experience meaningful and enduring successes is by one change or innovation at a time. We first lay strong foundational improvements or changes, upon which other incremental changes can be built upon.

For example, it would be very hard - and unsustainable to lose 50 pounds of body fat in 2 months. Not only would that be very hard, but it could also affect the way we take care of other areas of our lives given the extreme caloric restrictions needed to lose as much as 50 pounds in 2 months.

That's an example of a radical improvement or change.

Incremental change or improvements would mean breaking down our 50-pound target weight loss into 5 or 10 "goal chunks" of 10 or 5 pounds each, respectively, where we can aim to maximize our fat loss at 2 pounds per week only, which is the established healthy rate of fat loss.

After we achieve our first 5 to 10 pounds, we can call it a victory, take a short but healthy break and then go after the second 5 to 10-pound weight loss goal chunk. Doing it this way has 2 important benefits in terms of weight loss.

First, breaking our 50-pound weight loss goal into 5 to 10 smaller goal chunks makes the goal much more achievable and less intimidating. When our goals are like that, we can be highly encouraged to work on achieving them and feel confident about our ability to do so. And the more we feel like that, the higher our chances of successfully accomplishing our goals.

It's like choosing between having to put a 500-pound rock on top of the table in one try or breaking down that rock into 25 pieces weighing only 20 pounds each and placing those pieces 1 or 2 at a time on the table until we've successfully hauled all 500 pounds of that rock on top of the table. Now, isn't that easier and more realistic?

The second benefit of gunning for incremental improvements is motivation. By experiencing smaller but significantly more victories, we'll be able to build our confidence and motivation up with each incremental improvement to ourselves.

But more importantly, failing at something "small" doesn't have the same discouraging impact than failing at a big or grandiose goal. Compared to failing at making a very huge change in our life, failed attempts at much smaller changes or improvements won't depress us enough to keep us from trying again.

And occasional failures are a part of life, which makes them unavoidable. The only thing left for discussion is the impact such failures may have on us.

A very good example of this the benefits of gunning for incremental benefits as much as possible is when learning to speak a new language. According to www.fluentu.com, one of the keys to learning a new language as fast as possible is to focus on learning the "right" words for that language first instead of trying to learn as many words of a new language fast.

"Right" words refer to the words that comprise most of the sentences spoken during conversations of a specific language. For example, did you know that while the English language has anywhere from half a million to a million words in its vocabulary, the top 50% of texts in the English language are comprised of only the top 100 words, and 90% of English texts are comprised of just the top 1,000 words? That means if you're not an English-speaking person and you learn just 10 of the top 100 words of the English language every day, then you can learn to read and understand up to 50% of English language texts in just 10 days! And because you're only learning 10 new words daily, your chances of retaining them in your memory over the long term are much higher compared to if you went for 100 new words in a day.

Sustainability

Our chances of successfully making continuous personal improvements or changes over the long term - and achieving substantial successes in life - are much higher if we focus on consistently gunning for incremental self-improvements instead of occasional but radical changes.

A practical example of the sustainability of incremental self-improvements versus occasional radical ones is the Pomodoro technique, which I use to optimize my work productivity.

The Pomodoro technique involves working in 30-minute work cycles where I work for 25 straight minutes then take a mandatory 5-minute break at the end of the cycle, regardless of how energetic or tired I feel and during every 4th cycle, I extend the break to 10 minutes. When taking a break, I can do anything I want except for that which I'm working on.

I'll check out my social media accounts, take a walk or work on something else - anything but what I'm working on at that moment. The primary mechanism by which the Pomodoro technique works is breaking down a task into smaller chunks of 25-minute work times.

The reason for the mandatory breaks is to prevent the mind from getting exhausted prematurely and in the process, extend productivity time.

Before I learned this technique, I could only work for up to 5 hours daily. And by the end of the 5th hour, I'm too mentally exhausted to get anything else done.

But after using the Pomodoro technique, I was able to extend my productivity time to 7 hours max and got more work done. By working on a task in smaller increments, I was able to sustain such work for a much longer period of time.

In a sense, we can view the principle of incremental improvements or changes as similar to the Pomodoro technique in that it breaks down major changes or improvements in our lives into smaller and easier to accomplish chunks that don't overwhelm us mentally, which can allow us to sustain it over the long term.

Chapter 4 - S.M.A.R.T. Goal Setting

Now that we know why we should go for incremental improvements in key areas of our personal and professional lives, it's time to set goals for achieving those incremental improvements. It's tempting to think that goal setting is as simple as, well, setting goals.

But the truth is, it's not as simple as merely thinking of goals. It involves much more than that.

For us to be able to consistently achieve incremental self-improvements that will eventually add up to significant changes and successes in both our personal and professional lives, we'll need to set the right goals. We'll need to set SMART goals.

S.M.A.R.T.

The acronyms stand for specific, measurable, attainable, relevant, and timely - all of which are important characteristics of meaningful goals. Goals that are SMART have a much higher chance of being accomplished compared to dumb, I mean goals that aren't SMART.

As such, setting SMART goals are an important part of the Kaizen philosophy of continuous improvement.

Often times, SMART goal setting activities are done in the corporate or business world. But many people fail to apply SMART in their own lives and end up settling for lives that are hardly successful in both the personal and professional fronts.

No doubt about it, we can use the same SMART goal setting strategy as we live a Kaizen-based life, which is a life of continuous improvements.

Specific

A goal has to be clear and not ambiguous. Just as it's impossible to hit an unknown target (even if you already hit it, you won't know you did because you don't know it's a target), we can't hit or achieve goals that aren't clear or known to us. An example of an unclear or vague goal is "I want to be happy!" for a couple of reasons.

First, happy is relative. If you ask a beggar in the street, having 3 full meals a day and a one-bedroom flat is happiness! But if you ask an NBA player, being happy probably means having at least a $5 million annual paycheck playing for the Golden State Warriors.

Second, being happy is too general and can become a moving target because of random events. That's why it's important to be specific about what it means to be happy.

Is it getting married to your long-time love? Is it having a child? Or is it being promoted to the general manager position in your company?

Measurable

By measurable, it means a goal can be expressed in numbers so it becomes objective. In the examples above, how many children do you want to have? How many steps do you want to be promoted so you can become a general manager?

To the extent that you can measure goals is the extent you can objectively determine whether or not you've succeeded - or failed - to achieve them. And it can give you a much clearer picture as to how far you are from achieving your goals.

Attainable

This is possibly the most important characteristic of any goal you'll set and this is also probably the most debatable characteristic too. The reason why this may be the most important is because no matter how specific, measurable, relevant and time-bound your goals are, they all don't mean squat if they're impossible to attain.

For example, a goal of being able to play for the Golden State Warriors (specific) for at least 2 years (measurable) within the next 5 years (time-bound) because you're the star varsity basketball player of your university (relevant) but standing only 5 feet flat is an unrealistic or unattainable goal because of height or the lack of it.

If we constantly set unattainable goals for ourselves, we'll eventually get tired and discouraged from consistent failures to the point where we may think to ourselves "What's the point?" And when that happens, intentional self-improvement would become nothing but a memory.

Therefore, it's important that we set attainable or realistic goals for ourselves.

One of the best ways I know to set attainable goals is to ask ourselves: Are the results of these goals dependent on me or on other people or circumstances? If they're dependent on you, then the chances of achieving those goals are high because they're largely within your control.

If they're dependent on others or circumstances, chances are high that they're not attainable because it's dependent on other people or circumstances.

So instead of setting a goal such as to get promoted to general manager in the next 5 years, which is dependent on how your bosses will evaluate your performance, make it a goal to be able to exceed the targets set for you by your bosses by at least 20%.

Doing so will make your goals within your control and it will help raise your chances of being able to convince your bosses that you are worthy of being promoted to general manager.

Relevant

Related to being attainable, relevant goals are those that are lined up with your strengths or skills, which make them a much higher probability of being achieved, especially if they're within your control.

A goal of being able to conduct 1 paid personal finance talk for an audience of at least 20 people is relevant if you have a strong background in finance, but if you're a veterinarian by training, it's not a relevant goal.

However, you can attend seminars, classes or training sessions on personal finances so eventually, you'll be qualified to conduct such seminars. You can make attending such classes or seminars your first goal, which is relevant to your background as a veterinarian in this example.

And this is why incremental self-improvement is crucial. By building upon previous improvements you've already made, goals can be more relevant and thus, enjoy a higher probability of being accomplished.

Timely

The final component of meaningful or SMART goals is timeliness, i.e., being time-bound. Without setting a time-frame, it can be very easy to succumb to the temptation of procrastination because open-ended goals aren't urgent goals, which can be very tempting to put off for as long as possible.

And to set optimal timelines for goals, I highly recommend using Parkinson's Law, which I first learned of through Tim Ferris' bestselling book "The 4-Hour Workweek."

Parkinson's Law suggests that a task's or goal's perceived importance increases with shorter deadlines. In other words, giving your goals a relatively shorter deadline than expected or required can make you have a sense of urgency and focus that's needed not only to achieve your goals but also accomplishing them well because of the relatively increased focus.

When I used to write reports in the office, I made it a habit to set personal deadlines for finishing them that's at least 1 day earlier than the ones my bosses gave me.

It gave me a much greater sense of urgency and focus, which allowed me to significantly improve the quality of the reports I wrote, both in terms of minimized revisions and turnaround times.

Chapter 5 - Single Vs. Multi-Tasking

Have you ever had the impression that people who multi-task are much more productive compared to others who don't? After all, multitasking is akin to hitting multiple birds with just one time-stone, right? Wrong!

Multi-tasking is detrimental to productivity because it increases risks for mistakes and can suppress creative flow. Why is that so? The first reason is that multi-tasking isn't real - it's just an illusion. Consider the basis for the belief in multi-tasking: the mighty computer processor.

We all think because our computers and laptops are able to perform several tasks at a time - from loading a webpage to playing a video using another program - which it really is multi-tasking. But the truth is that computers don't perform tasks simultaneously.

Computers perform only one task at a time. The only reason why they appear to be capable of multi-tasking as we know it is because they're able to perform tasks at a very rapid pace and switch back and forth between tasks at very blinding speeds that the naked eye can't perceive.

They switch from one task to another so fast - think The Flash fast - that they appear to be doing several things at a time.

If computers aren't capable of multi-tasking – in line with what we think about multi-tasking - how can we puny humans be capable of it? Now you may make the case for multi-tasking by citing a circus juggler who's able to juggle multiple balls or bottles at a time.

That too is an illusion because jugglers function pretty much like computer processors in that they shift their focus or attention from once ball or bottle to another at a very rapid pace to the point that they appear to be multi-tasking! Jugglers rapidly shift their focus or attention from balls that they are about to throw in the air to balls that are already falling.

Ok, given that multi-tasking, at least in the computer and juggler contexts, is all about rapidly shifting from task to another, it appears that multi-tasking in such contexts appears to be something that's doable. Yes, it can be done. But the issue isn't whether or not it can be done. The question now - viewing multi-tasking from a new, focus-transitioning perspective - is whether or not it's a wise or productive practice. Why?

It's because we're not computers in the sense that we can easily switch our focus back and forth across mentally intensive tasks with skipping a beat.

Especially if we're juggling between two tasks that require a significant amount of focus such as writing a report and taking notes in class, shifting from one mentally-demanding task to another will require a mental adjustment period to get into the flow of the task to which we'll shift back to. And this can result in 2 things.

First, it will take us longer to finish a task. If we just focus on one task and finish it before moving on to the next mentally demanding one, we only need to "warm up" or get into "the flow" just once, which is at the beginning. Let's say for a particular task, it can take us up to 3 minutes to get into a good state of mental flow.

If we switch from and to such a task because of multi-tasking at least 5 times as we work to complete it, then we'll be adding at least 15 minutes to the work process, i.e., 3 minutes to get back into the flow for each of the 5 shifts.

And apart from the 3-minute period for getting back in the flow, switching from one task to another can add more time to the process because we'll have to re-connect what we need to do with what we already finished prior to the shifting. That's why it's not unusual for turnaround times to effectively double when multitasking, especially if the tasks involved require a lot of mental effort.

The second highly possible and unfavorable result of multitasking is a serious error. How many times have you come across drivers who get into fatal accidents because they we're trying to perform 2 mentally demanding tasks at a time, which are driving and texting.

Driving is a task that requires complete and undivided attention at all times. There's a very serious chance that within the 1 or 2 seconds that we shift our attention from the road in front of us to typing the right characters on our phones while composing a text message, another vehicle or worse, a person would cross in front the vehicle we're driving.

And with vehicular accidents, 1 to 2 seconds may be considered an eternity of time in which to happen.

Single-Tasking

This is one incremental self-improvement that can pay huge dividends down the road, one, which can open up many other doors for other incremental or continuous improvements both in our personal and professional lives.

This is because all incremental changes or improvements require serious focus to implement and sustain and single tasking - as compared to multi-tasking - is all about being in the moment and focusing on the task at hand.

There are several ways by which we can focus enough on one task at a time and accomplish them with flying colors as a result. The very first thing we'll need to do is block out a specific amount of time for a task and that task alone.

When we already know how much time we have, we can have a sense of urgency about it (remember Parkinson's Law?) and as a result, work with greater focus. And by blocking out time periods for each task, we can organize our work schedules better and minimize the risks of forgetting to work on them.

The second way we can focus on one task at a time - and accomplish them well - is by going off the grid. What I mean by this is going offline and putting our phones on silent or airplane mode.

This is to eliminate all possible distractions in order to preserve precious mental energy. You see, we draw from our mental energy reserves every time we have to use our willpower to ignore distractions or resist the temptation to pay attention to them.

If we're online and are readily accessible while working on a task, the chances of either getting distracted - and effectively reverting to multi-tasking - or depleting our willpower or mental reserves rapidly will be very high. And when our mental reserves are quickly drained, we won't have enough mental power to continue focusing and finishing a task.

But when we go offline and either put our phones on silent or airplane mode, we won't have to use up our mental or willpower reserves because there won't be any temptations to resist.

Another thing that can help us improve our ability to focus on tasks or improvements that we're working on is regular meditation. Meditation is what running or lifting weights in the gym is to the body and physical muscles. The mind can be considered as our mental muscle and meditation is an excellent way to work it out and make it stronger and more agile.

It takes a lot of mind power to be able to sit still and quiet the mind during meditation. If you don't believe me, try sitting still and think of nothing for just 2 minutes. You'll get my drift. That's why regular meditation helps make our minds much stronger and agile.

There are many ways to meditate from the extremely weird to the very practical and for purposes of developing a focus for successfully practicing the philosophy of Kaizen in our lives for personal and professional success, I'll share with you a very simple breathing-meditation technique that I learned from bestselling author and ex-Navy SEAL, Mark Divine. It's called the box-breathing technique.

To perform the box-breathing technique, sit in a comfortable and upright position with both hands on your lap. With your entire body relaxed, breathe deeply through the nose and with your belly (not your chest) for 5 seconds. Hold your breath for 5 seconds before exhaling through the nose for another 5 seconds.

Finally, hold the exhaled position for 5 seconds before repeating the whole box-breathing cycle again for a minimum of 10 minutes per session. Meditation can be done anytime of the day, but for best results, I highly recommend that you do it first thing in the morning - or at least within the first 90 minutes of your day - and to the extent possible, do it at the same time every day.

Box breathing works two ways: mentally and physiologically. Mentally, it trains your mind to pay attention to and focus on your breathing, which over time will make you focus on anything much better.

Physiologically, meditation techniques like this that involve slow and deep breathing help calm your nervous system and slow down your heart rate, which can help you focus and calm your mind better.

Chapter 6 - Organizational Kaizen

In this book, we're looking at how to practice the Kaizen philosophy for our personal gain, i.e., for personal and professional success. And to some extent, you will need the help of others - a team of people so to speak - to help you carry out important incremental and continuous improvements in order to succeed on both fronts.

In this chapter, we'll be talking about applying Kaizen within the context of an organizational structure, i.e., a company or a working unit, which is very important for professional success in more ways than one.

To be more specific, we'll talk about key principles we can use to lead teams of people in living the Kaizen philosophy at work so that our teams can successfully accomplish their goals through continuous improvements.

Leadership by Example

The best way to get people to follow and obey us is by leading through example. If we want your team members to take the Kaizen philosophy seriously within the team, we need to show them that we ourselves take it seriously. In other words, we'll need to walk the talk and practice what we preach.

This is because more is caught than taught. What this means is our actions do speak louder than words. As the Bible says in James 2:18, "*Show me your faith without deeds, and I will show you my faith by my deeds.*" People will believe us more and will want to follow us more if our words and our actions line up.

But if our words and actions go on separate ways, people will follow our actions more than our words. Remember, that words are nothing without action and if our actions consistently contradict what we tell our team members, our integrity will erode over time to the point where they may no longer follow what we ask them to do.

And when that happens, we can kiss Kaizen in our organization goodbye.

The Golden Rule

In case you forgot, the golden rule is "Do unto others what you want others to do unto you." The other side of the golden rule is "Don't do to others what you don't want them to do unto you." In other words, we can't expect others to relate to us - as a boss or team leader - with respect if we constantly talk down on them with little or no respect.

We can't expect our subordinates to follow our orders if we rebel against our respective bosses too. Respect begets respect and obedience begets the same.

Another thing worth doing to others that we also want to be done to us is being patient with shortcomings, especially if our subordinates acknowledge them and vow to do better. It's easy to lose patience with our subordinates when their shortcomings will backfire on us but if we consider how it feels when we're the ones who have shortchanged our respective superiors, it can become easier to be patient.

The more we treat our people the way we want to be treated, the more they'll support our efforts at implementing Kaizen in the organization, which means our chances of successfully leading our teams to making constant improvements that'll benefit the organization as a whole become higher as well. And when that happens, we can be appreciated even more by our superiors and the chances of us getting promoted can be much higher.

Foster Tolerance

Striving for constant improvement isn't an easy endeavor to sustain. As such, we'll need to encourage and empower our team members to be proactive and place the same value as we have on constantly improving the way we do things in our teams or in our organizations. For this, it's crucial that we're able to foster a sense of emotional security among our team members.

It's only when members of our team feel emotionally secure can they feel comfortable speaking out and giving their opinions on how things are done in the team, which may give us valuable information for constantly improving the way our teams operate.

One of the most important characteristics of teams with relatively secure members is an atmosphere of tolerance. By tolerance, I mean being open to new ideas, especially divergent or seemingly critical ones, on how things can be improved within our teams and ultimately, our organizations as a whole. Creativity and innovation thrive best within an environment of tolerance, i.e., open-mindedness, and are necessary for successfully implementing the Kaizen philosophy in our work teams.

One thing I have to clarify about regarding the cultivation of a tolerant work environment is that it doesn't mean we won't correct mistakes or call the attention of team members who aren't acting in line with the team or company's policies and guidelines.

Continuous improvements require continuous corrections of erroneous or unproductive practices and attitudes. The key to successfully correcting our people and ensure continuous improvements is respectfully calling their attention and giving them the chance to explain themselves.

By doing so, we can make them feel that they are being heard and that they're not judged quickly. This can help foster emotional security among our team members, which is crucial for consistently being able to improve things in our organizations and our teams.

Focus On What Can Be Done

While constant improvement requires consistently identifying "wrong" or "inefficient" practices or processes in the work place, the main goal is to find ways to address, minimize, or eliminate them on an incremental basis. And this means we must focus on finding solutions that can effectively address the challenges or situations that our teams and organizations face instead of focusing on determining who's at fault.

I'm not saying that finding out who's ultimately responsible isn't important because it is. Otherwise, how will we know who to correct or encourage in order to minimize or eliminate the re-occurrence of unproductive or negative situations and challenges?

Focus Mostly On Changing Processes Instead Of People

One of the things that can help us a lot in terms of minimizing our tendency to blame our team members is focusing on what's wrong with our team's processes, i.e., how our teams do things.

We should take great effort in exposing "loopholes" or gaps in our team's processes and practices instead of looking for people to blame and correcting them. Why? It's because if we have very good systems in place, there will very little room for human or judgment errors or willful violations of team or organizational policies and rules.

In contrast, if we focus on correcting the people at fault, we may continue to leave gaps or loopholes in our team or organization's processes and make it highly likely for certain violations or problems to manifest again even after correcting or replacing the people responsible.

For this, it'd be good to ask "Why?" at least 3 to 5 times in order to get to the root of the problem - to discover the real loopholes or gaps in the way our teams operate so we can plug the right holes and prevent such holes from manifesting again. Now, isn't that what Kaizen or constant improvements are all about?

Publicize Exceptional Performance

One of the best leadership practices that can help foster a strong sense of loyalty and dedication among our team members is to exalt them in public and rebuke them in private. It's basic human nature to desire being valued and commended in front of other people and being corrected or rebuked without anybody else around.

So if our team members were able to achieve something praiseworthy, it would be great to announce it to the rest of the team and if by their teamwork the team was able to successfully help the team improve an area of its operations, we should announce it to the whole team as well.

Doing so will help foster a deep sense of loyalty, satisfaction, and pride in being part of our team and a well-motivated team is a very valuable asset when it comes to successfully living out the Kaizen philosophy in any organization.

Chapter 7 - Maximizing Your Kaizen Results

As we end, allow me to share with you several important principles for making the most out of our Kaizen efforts. By keeping these key principles of continuous improvement in mind, we can greatly increase our chances of being able to experience massive successes in our personal and professional lives.

Identify

Continuous professional and personal improvements won't be possible if we don't have an idea of what we need to improve on! And truth is, it's hard to be able to objectively identify the things we need to improve on in our lives because of two things: bias and lack of awareness.

And here's where empowering others, which we discussed in Chapter 2 can be very helpful. People who know us so well and who we trust greatly are in very good positions to see the things that we need to improve on - things that may be holding us back from taking off and experiencing great success in our lives.

They have the benefit of objectivity and perspective, which are both lacking in us when it comes to properly identifying our areas for improvement.

We should take the time to reflect on our perceived areas for improvement and ask for other people's feedback on the same. Then, we should carefully study our perceived areas for improvement and those that others give us, so we can have a much clearer picture of the areas of our lives that need to be improved.

Plan

It's been said that failing to plan is planning to fail. Identifying our weak spots don't mean much if we don't have a strategy to deal with them. For effective planning, I highly recommend setting SMART goals that will directly address the areas we identified - together with other people - for improvement. And we should always keep in mind that such goals must be those that are largely if not completely within our control to accomplish.

The accomplishment of such goals shouldn't be dependent on other people or circumstances.

Implement

Plans, like identified areas for improvement, are practically worthless without effective implementation. And for this, we may need to seek the help of people we trust.

It's because there will be times when we don't have the resources, expertise, experience, or willpower to do the things necessary for continuous improvement but other people have them. There's no shame in asking for help.

And even if we feel that we're perfectly capable of doing the necessary things for constant improvement, we can still benefit by asking key people to be our accountability partners, i.e., people who'll hold us responsible or accountable for not being able to accomplish what needs to be accomplished.

The pressure from knowing that we have authorized other people to hold us responsible for our continuous improvement efforts can be a strong motivation for giving it our best and avoid procrastination.

Evaluate

After implementing our continuous improvement efforts for a period of time, we'll need to step back and evaluate our progress in those areas of our personal and professional lives that we are working to improve on. And for this, it's important that we document the results of our efforts, whether in qualitative or quantitative form.

The advantage of being able to measure or document our progress in quantitative form, i.e., using numbers, is that numbers don't lie and are objective. If we're working to improve our physical stamina through running, we can use running apps like RunKeeper or Strava to document or record our running performances, i.e., speed, distance, and duration, among others.

By comparing our running sessions' data on duration, distance, and speed, we can objectively determine whether or not we're progressing or digressing.

But of course, not all progress can be quantified. That's where journaling can also come in handy. For example, if we're working on improving the quality of our sleep, the primary benchmark for evaluating whether or not we're progressing is how we feel the following day.

And we can compare how we feel over the next few days after implementing new sleep quality improvement strategies by writing down our sleeping times and how we felt the days after.

It would also help a lot to have other people - our accountability partners - help us in evaluating our progress. As mentioned earlier, they can provide us with the benefit of being more objective and less biased.

We may evaluate our progress more highly than we ought to or we can be so hard on ourselves and grossly underestimate the progress we've already made. Having a fresh pair of eyes to help us with our evaluation can help minimize the risks for either error.

Adjust Accordingly

Finally, we'll need to act in accordance with our progress or digress evaluation.

Much like the necessity of having to stop over once in a while when driving from one end of the United States to the other along the Interstate to check if we're still on the right path or if we've veered off, we'll also need to do the same when it comes to our constant self-improvement endeavors.

Otherwise, we run the risk of not being able to successfully implement the incremental changes or improvements needed for a successful personal and professional life.

Conclusion

Thank you for buying this book. I hope that through this, you've learned a lot about how the Kaizen philosophy of continuous improvement can help you experience great successes in both your personal and professional life. But knowing is only half the battle for personal and professional success, my friend. The other half is action or application of knowledge.

That's why I highly encourage you to apply in your own life what you learned in this book. And the best way to do it, consistent with the incremental change principle of Kaizen, is to apply one or two learnings at a time.

Small changes for big and lasting success will always trump radical changes that are highly unrealistic and unsustainable.

Again, remember that Rome wasn't built in a day but the Romans were busy laying bricks every hour. That's the essence of continuous or incremental improvements.

That's the essence of Kaizen.

Here's to your many incremental successful life improvements my friend! Cheers!

References:

1. https://www.developgoodhabits.com/kaizen-continuous-improvement/
2. https://www.success.com/blog/the-importance-of-constant-self-improvement
3. https://ph.kaizen.com/about-us/definition-of-kaizen.html
4. https://www.kanbanchi.com/what-is-kaizen
5. https://www.bmilab.com/blog/2017/8/3/two-strategic-approaches-to-innovation-incremental-vs-radical
6. https://www.wired.com/insights/2013/11/the-power-of-incremental-innovation/
7. https://www.makeuseof.com/tag/single-vs-multitasking-whats-best-productivity/
8. https://agileleanlife.com/kaizen-rules-for-teams/
9. http://fortune.com/2016/12/07/why-you-shouldnt-multitask/
10. https://www.fluentu.com/blog/fastest-way-to-learn-a-new-language/